Asia

Europe

Africa

Australia

A Ride on

Mother's Back

A DAY OF BABY CARRYING
AROUND THE WORLD

WRITTEN BY Emery Bernhard

ILLUSTRATED BY Durga Bernhard

Gulliver Books

Harcourt Brace & Company

SAN DIEGO   NEW YORK   LONDON

Text copyright © 1996 by Emery Bernhard
Illustrations copyright © 1996 by Durga Bernhard

Library of Congress Cataloging-in-Publication Data
Bernhard, Emery.
A ride on mother's back: a day of baby carrying around the world/
Emery & Durga Bernhard.—1st ed.
p. cm.
"Gulliver Books."
Includes notes.
Summary: Explores the ways in which people from a variety of cultures
carry their young ones, and describes what children see and learn as
they are carried.
ISBN 0-15-200870-5
1. Infant carriers—Cross-cultural studies—Juvenile literature.
2. Children—Cross-cultural studies—Juvenile literature. [1. Infant
carriers. 2. Cross-cultural studies. 3. Manners and customs.
4. Babies.] I. Bernhard, Durga. II. Title.
GT2467.B47   1996
392′.13—dc20   95-41483

Printed in Singapore

First edition
F E D C B A

The paintings in this book were done in Winsor & Newton gouache
on Whatman 140-lb. cold-press watercolor paper.
This book was printed with soya-based inks on Leykam recycled paper,
which contains more than 20 percent postconsumer waste and has
a total recycled content of at least 50 percent.
The text type was set in Fairfield Medium.
The display type was set in Worcester Round.
Color separations by Bright Arts, Ltd., Singapore
Printed and bound by Tien Wah Press, Singapore
Production supervision by Warren Wallerstein and Ginger Boyer
Designed by Lydia D'moch

To our parents:
Ruth and George, May and Jack

All around the world babies love to be held close. And parents everywhere need their hands free to work and play. Lifted and carried by someone who cares, young children ride into the day.

How do different peoples carry their babies?
What is it like to ride on mother's back?

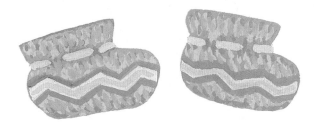

It is a chilly dawn in the mountains of Guatemala. Smoke from the fire hangs in the air, curling up into the blackened thatch roof of the hut. Newborn Rosha snuggles in the folds of the shawl tied around her mother. She rides safe and warm, close to her mother's body. Rosha nurses and sleeps, nurses and sleeps.

PAT, PAT, PAT. Rosha is rocked in the shawl as her mother pats corn dough and presses it into flat, round cakes. The fire crackles under the clay griddle, and one by one the tortillas puff up. Rosha hears her father and brothers talking while they sharpen their axes and hoes. They kiss Rosha's soft hair and say good-bye before starting their day of work.

It is just after sunrise on the island of Bali, and already the village is bustling. Farmers herd flocks of ducks toward the rice paddies. Women on their way to market carry baskets filled with dried fish and breadfruits and bananas. Many babies are carried down the narrow lane, including Wayan and Ketut.

The three-month-old twins ride in slings tied around their sisters' shoulders. They pass a neighbor trying to lead home a huge swaybacked pig that has escaped through a broken fence. The pig waddles along with its stomach nearly touching the ground, grunting loudly and sniffing at everyone going by.

Bonyo lives in the rain forest of central Africa. He is riding in a sling on Grandfather's hip. Suddenly a harsh whistle comes from the forest. Bonyo's father has found a honeybee hive!

Grandfather carries Bonyo toward the sound of the honey flute. The men are gathering at the bottom of a tall fig tree. They work together, helping Bonyo's father climb the tree and smoke out the bees. Leaf baskets filled with honeycombs are lowered to the ground. Everyone gets to taste the honey. Now Bonyo knows why everyone gets excited when they hear the honey flute!

Zuher rides in a cloth wrap knotted around his busy big sister. He watches while his sister and mother take down their tent and load their belongings onto a camel. The camel crouches down and waits, slowly chewing a mouthful of hay. Because the animals have eaten almost all the grass nearby, it is time for Zuher's tribe to move on to the next pasture in the Sahara.

Zuher sees the older children racing donkeys across the oasis. They shout at Zuher's sister as they ride across the bright sand. One day Zuher will ride the donkeys too. For now he is happy to be carried from place to place and to munch the bread his sister hands him.

On a frozen inlet in the Canadian far north, baby Pelagie nestles inside the large hood of her mother's parka. Her mother chops a hole in the ice with a long pole, and Pelagie giggles as she is bounced up and down. She peers over her mother's shoulder when her mother kneels down and points at the dark shapes moving in the water.

Pelagie's mother waits patiently for a tug on her baited line while Pelagie watches their husky puppy nosing about in the snow. The puppy bounds over and licks her face. A frigid wind whips over the low ridges, but mother and child are warm inside their caribou-skin clothing.

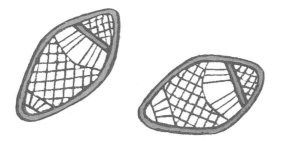

It is midday near the coast of West Africa. Tumani's mother
returns from the well with Tumani tied onto her back and a
heavy bowl of water balanced on her head. Lulled by his mother's
steady gait and soft humming, Tumani has fallen asleep.

SPLASH! . . . Tumani opens his eyes in time to see a stream
of water pouring into a tall jar set in the shade of a mango tree.
The air is heavy with dust and the sun is strong. Mother unties
the bright cloth wrap. It is time for Tumani to play with the
other children while the women of the village rest under the
old tree. Tumani begins to clap along with a circle of girls who
are clapping and singing in the shade.

Mai rests on her grandmother's back, secured with woven cloth. A few drops of cold rain fall from passing clouds over the high hills of Thailand, but Mai remains cozy against her grandmother. Grandmother takes care of Mai while Mai's mother sews colorful story cloths.

Mai is jiggled as her grandmother sifts rice with a shallow basket. The wind helps by blowing away the grassy chaff. Grandmother begins to tell the story about Mai's mother—when *she* was a little girl—who was taught by *her* grandmother to sew beautiful story cloths.

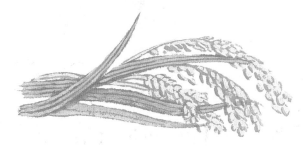

The jungle is steamy along the Amazon River. Davi is carried against his mother's hip, held in place by a cloth sash looped around her shoulder. Heading home to prepare dinner, Mother also carries a basket full of plantains from her garden. She walks so smoothly, moving without a sound on the spongy rain forest floor, that the shy deer nibbling on leaves near the trail do not run away.

Mother stops to gather the sweet seedpods of a kapok tree. She shows Davi the coiled snake draped in loops along a nearby branch and a scaly armadillo digging for insects. By the time Davi can walk, he too will move without a sound and will know all the ways of the forest.

Sita's family comes to Kathmandu each year to celebrate the beginning of spring at the festival of Holi. Crowds jam the plazas and marketplaces as musicians play and dancers parade. During the festival the people of Nepal also celebrate by sprinkling red powder, squirting colored water, and throwing water balloons at one another.

Sita rides in a sling on her father's back, holding a small bag of red powder. When colored water showers down on her, Sita closes her eyes and tries to duck. Then she opens her eyes and throws red powder back at the children passing by. The sweet smell of incense mingles with the sharp odor of curry. Of all the foods she tries today, Sita likes fried sugar candy the most!

It is hot in the highlands of Papua New Guinea. Gogomo sways in the cool net bag that hangs from his mother's head. Near the river Mother stops to gather firewood in another, larger net bag. She hears splashing and shouting. Men from the village are spearing fish while children search among the rocks for tadpoles.

Gogomo's mother loops the handle of the larger net bag over her head. Carrying Gogomo in front and the firewood on her back, she is ready to go home. Thunder rumbles in the distance. Soon it will begin to rain. Gogomo is hungry, but he must wait until he and his mother reach the shelter of their small hut. Then he can nestle in his mother's arms and nurse.

High in the Andes Mountains of South America, Juanita rides in a warm woolen shawl tied around her mother's strong shoulders. From far away on the thin, cold air come the sounds of sheep bleating and hooves clattering on rocks. The sun is setting.

Juanita's mother picks up a lamb that needs help keeping up with the herd. Juanita reaches to pet the lamb's wooly head. She watches the way her brother moves among the sheep, herding them closer to home. Juanita's brother plays a song on his flute and she hums along. Someday Juanita will herd the sheep and sing the songs she learned while riding on her mother's back.

Families carry their babies all through the day, while planting and harvesting, tending and gathering, cooking and playing. Snuggled and cuddled, jiggled and bounced, bundled and rocked, babies discover the world they live in.

And when evening comes and children are carried to bed in loving arms, their dreams will carry them through the night— until a new day begins.

Notes About the Peoples in This Book

For thousands of years people around the world have carried their babies in animal skins, cloth slings, and woven wraps. Today mothers often carry their nursing infants in fabric slings made with buckles and loops, or pack their toddlers in backpacks with metal frames. Babies learn about the world by being carried around in it, and we can learn about a culture by finding out how its people carry their babies. Here is some more information about the people in this book, and where and how they live.

In ancient times Rosha's people, the **Maya (MY-uh)**, established a great empire that stretched through much of Central America. They now live in farming communities organized around central villages in the highlands of Guatemala and Mexico. Many of the men work the land, often using simple tools like hoes or digging sticks. Corn, beans, and squash, which are staples of the Mayan diet, have been cultivated in Central America for at least five thousand years. Mayan women cook, clean, and weave clothing with elaborate designs.

When they are about seven years old, boys may begin learning to farm by helping in the fields, using small hoes. Young girls are busy making tortillas, fetching water and firewood, caring for the pigs and chickens, leading the sheep to graze, and practicing weaving on portable looms.

Wayan and Ketut live on the island of Bali, which is part of Indonesia. As three-month-old babies, the twins have never been put down on the ground. The **Balinese (Bah-li-NEEZ)** believe that babies are born pure and close to heaven, and that babies' feet should not touch the earth until they are 105 days old. At that age babies are given a ceremonial welcome and finally allowed to play on the ground.

Balinese men farm and maintain village buildings and temples. Women help farm, keep house, and run the markets. Both men and women are involved in the creation of arts and crafts, and in rituals that include elaborate dance, costumes, and music. The children of Bali love to fly kites. The islanders build handmade kites of many fanciful designs, some of them hundreds of feet long. Kite festivals are often held along the breezy beaches.

Bonyo's people, the **Mbuti (em-BOOD-ee)**, are one of about ten groups of nomadic peoples of central Africa. They move their homes from place to place in the rain forest, searching for animals to hunt and beehives to raid for honey. The Mbuti, who were once called Pygmies, live in sapling-and-leaf huts in small camps that are relocated approximately every month, or when food is scarce. Honey is valued not only for its taste, but also because it is traded for food and goods from outside the forest. The Mbuti trade with neighboring farmers, exchanging honey, meat, and labor for fresh vegetables, cookware, and clothing.

In an Mbuti hunting camp there is always someone, often an elder, keeping an eye on children like Bonyo. The children play all day long. They also learn the stories, songs, and dances of their people.

Zuher's people are constantly on the move. The **Tuareg (TWAH-reg)** are peaceful traders and nomadic cattle herders of the south-central Sahara Desert in northern Africa. Over the course of a year, they move their livestock from one pasture to the next as the seasons and grazing conditions change. The Tuareg sell a few of their animals whenever they need to buy grain, clothing, or other necessities. Older Tuareg children help care for the goats, cattle, and sheep that provide milk and the donkeys and camels that provide transportation.

Tuareg tents are made of animal skins, reed mats, and occasionally plastic, supported by poles. Whenever possible, the Tuareg set up their tents near a tree and use its limbs for storage. The bread that Zuher likes to eat is round and flat and made from millet and wild seed. It is part of the basic Tuareg diet, along with milk, cheese, and millet porridge.

Pelagie's people, the **Inuit (I-noo-ut)**, are natives of Greenland and the North American arctic. The name Inuit means "the people." These great hunters of caribou, seal, and walrus have managed not only to survive but to prosper in one of the coldest places on earth.

The Inuit continue to obtain meat and skin from the caribou they hunt. Ice fishing also provides an important winter food source, and berry picking during the short arctic summer supplies something traditionally rare in the Inuit diet—fresh fruit. But the Inuit have also adapted to modern ways. Now they can buy fruit in markets, and they live in houses as well as tents and igloos. When hunting, they may ride on snowmobiles as well as dogsleds. And many young Inuit attend public schools during the week and learn to hunt and fish on the weekends.

Tumani's people, the **Mandingo (man-DING-go)**, live in the grassy plains of West Africa. They are descended from the empire of Mali, which flourished for centuries along the Niger River. The Mandingo are mostly farmers or traders. In rural areas they often live in circular homes with thatch roofs grouped behind stake fences.

While Mandingo men are busy farming in the fields, many of the women tie their babies in bright cloth wraps and carry them as they go about their work. Babies watch their mothers thresh groundnuts or pound millet, prepare a meal or make jewelry. From an early age Mandingo children learn the complex songs and rhythms that accompany daily activities as well as special rituals and celebrations.

Mai and her family are **Hmong (MUNG)**, mountain-dwelling people who live on the steep highland slopes of Laos, Thailand, and northern Vietnam in Southeast Asia. Hmong babies are carried while their families farm the fields, mill corn, thresh rice, feed their chickens and pigs, and gather wild herbs.

The hardworking Hmong must relocate their villages of bamboo-and-thatch huts whenever the thin mountain soil washes away in the monsoon rains or is no longer fertile. Their traditions of embroidery and appliqué travel with them wherever they go. Hmong refugees in the United States continue to hand sew tapestries that illustrate both the old and the new stories of their people.

Davi's people are the **Yanomama (yah-no-MA-ma).** They live in the Amazon rain forest of Venezuela and northern Brazil in South America. The Yanomama clear patches in the forest where they build large circular huts using leaves, vines, and wood. Yanomama families live together in groups that number from fifty to one hundred people, and the children learn from everyone around them. All food is shared among the people as if they were one big family.

Everyone helps harvest the gardens that grow plantains, bananas, and sugarcane. Women also fish and gather firewood and edible plants, while men hunt game animals such as monkeys, armadillos, rabbits, and tapir. At a young age boys are given small bows and arrows so they can practice their hunting skills.

Sita's family is **Nepali (nuh-PAW-lee).** They live in a village nestled among the Himalayan Mountains of southern Asia. Like most Nepali, Sita and her family practice a form of Hinduism.

Village people may walk a long way to reach a city in Nepal. This landlocked country is rugged and overcrowded, and walking is still a common way to travel. A visit to Kathmandu for the springtime Hindu festival of Holi is a special occasion for the rural farmers of Nepal. They come to pray to the young god Krishna, and also to feast, listen to music, watch the dancers, and trade and shop in the markets. Red is a sacred color used not only during Holi, but also in much of Nepali religious art and decoration.

Gogomo is a native of the large island of Papua New Guinea, which is north of Australia. Many **Papuans (PA-puh-wuns)** still live in simple, thatched stilt-houses in villages in the rain forests. They garden, catch fish, hunt large birds, and gather wild fruits, nuts, and vegetables. They also raise pigs for ceremonial feasts. In many villages men and women still live in separate houses. Young boys like Gogomo live with their mothers and sisters.

The Papuans are known around the world for their carvings and masks. Each village has its own style of carving. Another important craft is weaving. Papuans weave dried leaves and grass to make house walls, sleeping mats, and baskets. The net bag that Gogomo is carried in is woven with string made from the inner bark of trees.

Juanita's family are **Quechua (KE-chuh-wuh),** descendants of the Inca empire, a South American civilization that thrived centuries ago. Most Quechua-speaking Indians now live in the Andes Mountains of Peru and Bolivia, where they farm the steep, rocky land. Their small, one- or two-room homes are made with mud, stone, or brick, with roofs of grass, tile, or metal sheets. The Quechua depend on their small herds of sheep for wool and meat.

The Quechua make beautiful folk art quilts as well as richly colored woven shawls and ponchos, knit hats, and sweaters. The haunting music of their flutes, drums, and stringed instruments has also become famous, and is one of the highlights of the annual carnival celebration in the Andes.

A baby rides on his mother's back in a cradleboard at a powwow.
Once widely used by Native American mothers, cradleboards
are now mainly used for ceremonial purposes.

Greenland

North America